PREPARED BY GOD

THE SOURCE NOT MADE FROM MAN

By

Nadine Sallins

Prepared by God

The Source Not Made From Man

Copyright 2021 by Nadine Sallins

All rights reserved. No part of this publication may be reproduced, distributed, or transmitted in any form or by any means, including photocopying, recording, or other electronic or mechanical methods, without the prior written permission of the publisher, except in the case of brief quotations embodied in critical reviews and certain other noncommercial uses permitted by copyright law.

Although the author and publisher have made every effort to ensure that the information in this book was correct at press time, the author and publisher do not assume and hereby disclaim any liability to any party for any loss, damage, or disruption caused by errors or omissions, whether such errors or omissions result from negligence, accident, or any other cause.

Adherence to all applicable laws and regulations, including international, federal, state, and local governing professional licensing, business practices, advertising, and all other aspects of doing business in the US, Canada or any other jurisdiction is the sole responsibility of the reader and consumer.

Neither the author nor the publisher assumes any responsibility or liability whatsoever on behalf of the consumer or reader of this material. Any perceived slight of any individual or organization is purely unintentional.

The resources in this book are provided for informational purposes only and should not be used to replace the specialized training and professional judgment of a health care or mental health care professional.

Neither the author nor the publisher can be held responsible for the use of the information provided within this book. Please always consult a trained professional before making any decision regarding treatment of yourself or others.

Dedication

Lord

(Jesus Christ)

I appreciate your love that you proved to me, all the way to cavalry.

The stripes, the nails, the wounds I see, in you I have the victory.

Introduction

Many times, you will hear how God comes to the rescue and many times you will see how people come to God and how the tables are turned in their lives for the good. I am one of those people who not only had my tables turned but they are still turning. My table is never ending and to understand why and how, is shown in my story.

Times were tough, times were hard, but nothing can be compared to how God came and turned everything right side up. Including me. A follower of Christ, a child of God, and a person whose life purpose was to show you how to overcome, how to get the help from the source that is not found in man. Especially not in our own works but nevertheless a story written for you.

Here is to you, the story of a woman who became a role model for the rejected, the overlooked and the abused. While my story will allow you to follow me, it also leads you to who you really need to follow. Jesus Christ.

Chapter One

In the Beginning

On August 11, 1970, my mother gave birth to a healthy baby girl and named her Nadine, which means "hope." Coming up and being raised as a newborn I do not remember much about but as I grew in age things started to become clearer. I would love to say that I had a "perfect life" but that would not be the truth because no one is perfect, BUT GOD.

Throughout my years of becoming what God created me to be, I can say it was not what I would call "the easy life." *(John 16 :33) (Hebrews 12 :7) however, his grace was sufficient.* Finally realizing years down the line, it was very comforting to know my life was centered around him.

My grandmother had 10 children, a believer in Christ, a pastor, and strong black woman who loved God. She spent most of her life wanting to please God in serving, standing for and honoring his precepts and statutes in her way of living, wanting her life to reflect the things that would give him honor.

I remember, I used to look in the sky and I was infatuated by the clouds. I would just stare and be stuck just looking up. "So beautiful" I would say, "No man could have gotten up there and made those clouds like that, so beautiful." At that moment in my mind, it dawned on me Something is up there that cannot be explained, only a supernatural source that could not be from a man." (2nd Corinthians 4:7).

From then on, I remember watching my grandmother and as she prayed for people and how she opened the Bible to read, or to give a scripture as an encouragement to someone that God was in control, and that nothing takes him by surprise, (Romans 8:28). I remember watching and listening to my grandmother preach in the church. One thing about my grandmother she made sure everybody that lived in her household got up and went to church, it was not a matter of how you were feeling. Those were her rules, no exceptions, (Psalm 150:6).

I had aunts and uncles that were Pastors. A few are still living, and some have transitioned. I can say that I was blessed to be raised in a family who love the Lord and the opportunity to know him as my personal savior later in life, (Isaiah 45:22).

I remember, just like it was yesterday, I was around ten years old sitting on the staircase in my grandmother's house. We were living there with her at the time. It was nighttime and my cousin suffered from Epilepsy. He was having an episode that night. I remember I was frightened because I had never experienced anyone going through a seizure. I was shocked and scared; my grandmother had a Bible in her hand, and I remember one of my cousins laying on the couch and my grandmother reading the bible over him. She was praying and laying the Bible and her hands-on top of his chest speaking the word as he was having the seizure. It was just like a few minutes after she prayed, and she did not stop praying but as she continued praying, you could see something was happening and shortly following all of my grandmother's prayers he came out of it. Wow! I said to myself "What was that?" She prayed and things started happening. She spoke the word and laid it on his chest, and he came out of it. At the age of 10 seeing what I just saw was something that seemed unreal. I do not even remember anyone else around but me and my grandmother and my cousin, shocked and amazed. I had no understanding of what just happened, but I was so glad when it stopped. (Mark 16 :17).

Throughout the time I lived with my grandmother I learned a lot. I used to put on her high heels and try to walk in them the way she did. She was so funny; her life was centered around God and the atmosphere that was set around her was amazing. You knew when you walked into her home or room that she loved the Lord, her life also had that reflection. She was not perfect, but again none of us are. I love and miss her so much. It is good to know she is resting peacefully with our heavenly father. She carried her cross all the way until she transitioned. I didn't understand at the time, but I know in the bible Jesus says, "in order to follow him we must deny ourselves and take up our cross daily." (Matthew 16:24). I had a front row seat in that experience as she carried her cross.

So many memories of my grandmother I can remember, but no matter what you were going through she always had a way to make you laugh through your pain. Watching her as she prayed for her children as they went through the issues of life. And when she prayed, things changed. Nobody but God could make those kinds of things happen, (psalm 127:1). You could see the daily miracles clearly.

Chapter 2

Since the Beginning

My mom, my siblings and I did not have much, but we were grateful for what we had. We didn't have a choice. We learned to appreciate what was already on the table and I am thankful to God for that. My mother had six children, five living and one transitioned shortly after birth. I love my mother so much; she is the apple of my eye. So strong, loving, and strict on certain things. I don't blame her for being strict raising five children to be exact, I'm quite sure it was not easy. I thank God for her and the strength he gave her.

My relationship with my brothers and sisters, you can say was "out of the ordinary." We loved each other and we still do. Like most siblings we have our ups and downs. Living under the same roof, we had our share of arguments and disagreements like any other normal family, and I remember saying, "I can't wait until I get my own place."

I was molested twice at the age of 11 years old by a close relative and a friend of my relative. This happened a few times. The last occurrence was one of the most horrible days of my life. Through the abuse I was injured internally and had to see a doctor. This allowed me to reveal what was going on to my mother. Finally, I could talk about it. My parents went to the parents of this other person's home and they handled the situation and the abuse stopped. Looking back in hindsight, it was the fear that kept me from telling or getting help sooner. Not knowing what or how to tell someone this was going on was so much from fear. If I could tell anyone reading this book that if you or anyone you know is in this situation, TELL SOMEONE, NO MATTER WHAT! A teacher, neighbor, caregiver in your family, church member or another adult.

This whole ordeal left me disturbed mentally during my years in school, this reflected in my behavior. I was angry and was always in fights at school from others picking on me. This resulted in suspensions and disciplinary actions when I got home. I felt bad because I was only defending myself when I was picked on, but I was always the one blamed and never started the fight. I received beatings from my father, he and my mother couldn't understand why this was a continual thing with me in school. These beatings came due to the fights and suspensions in school or when I had arguments with my siblings. We would get into a fight and I would get a beating for scratching one of them in the face. I was so terrified whenever I got into trouble. My mother would tell my father what happened, and I would get a beating. No one believed me. It seemed like I was always starting something and got what they thought I deserved. I didn't start anything with anyone. It was always the other person and when they hit me, I hit them back and that's how the fight started but I was always blamed. I did not understand, I just "turn the other cheek" like the scripture mentions in the bible. Even at that age. I had so much going on inside me, being violated and all. Not sure what to do with all these emotions, I just kept putting them deep down inside of me.

Later at the age of 12 years old I was called downstairs to be introduced to someone. My mother claimed, "This is your real father"??? with a confused face. I shook his hand, said, "hello" and went back upstairs.

I didn't understand. The (first) father that took me out, brought my school clothes, fed me, beat my behind for getting in trouble in school, was not my "biological father?" I didn't know who this new man was. I never saw him before. Where did he come from, and why is he just turning up now? Why wasn't I told? So many questions with no answers to follow.

I kept quiet and just considered it to be so since that is what I was being told. As weeks and months grew, we started getting to know each other. I would see him across the street, and he would come and give me money. We would talk for a minute. I said, "Thanks dad" and left. We didn't see each other often just every now and then. The last time we spoke he said, "He was going to come and get me for the weekend to stay over at his house to meet his wife and my two half-sisters." One from his previous marriage and his stepdaughter. I said, "ok" and I started visiting on the weekends.

I met his wife and my two half-sisters, but it seemed as if his wife didn't care for me so much. There were rumors floating around about me. She was telling people that I only came around because I wanted money. Isn't a father supposed to support his daughter? I thought so. Why didn't she like me? What did I do to her to give her the impression that I only wanted money? I was only a child. As time went on, she made me feel very uncomfortable during visits and I didn't want to stay over anymore. I said nothing to anyone when I got back home.

His wife would be drinking alcohol and saying things about my father that I thought should have been kept between her and him. There were times I stayed over, and they were arguing, and she would be crying. I just felt so uncomfortable. She started treating me mean when he was not around, but then when he returned, it was like she pretended to tolerate me. I never told my father because I didn't want to hurt him. I never heard him say one bad word about her. He really loved her, and I didn't want to cause any problems, so I kept quiet.

I was accused of not calling him or coming to visit but how do you tell your father your wife hates me and treats me like trash when you're not around. Tell me how? He worshiped the ground she walked on and I never wanted to come over to visit anymore because prior visits and overnight stays led to a lot of things being spilled out through intoxication of some sort. Especially about his drinking and reliance on her and what he didn't have and what was hers.

I had nothing to do with their marriage. I did not want to stay over there anymore because of the lies and gossip I had to listen to. I separated myself from them and didn't see him for a while. The last time I saw him was two days before he passed away.

Chapter 3

Truth Be Told

I felt sold off like a slave for money, (1 Tim 6:10) and was led to believe that my (biological) father passed away, but God said, "NOT SO." My biological father was revealed to me by God. When my actual biological father was revealed, I really questioned why then did I attend the funeral of a man my mom claimed to be my "Biological father" if he was not my father?

Again, humiliated, and embarrassed. I was not even mentioned in the obituary and I was not acknowledged at all as his daughter. I was devastated. The man God revealed to me as my biological dad was right there at the funeral and it wasn't the one being lowered into the ground in the casket. He helped carry the casket, he was one of the pallbearers.

They all looked at me like I was crazy at the burial as I screamed out loud as they lowered the casket, "rest in peace daddy, I love you." No one said anything as I walked away crying feeling so alone and deceived not even being recognized. All that, to later find out that he was not my father, but my real father was right there watching everything. Lost for words, I just left. For years I tossed and turned in my bed at night in tears as I cried out to God, "WHY?" I did not ask to be here, but I know now God had a plan for my life, (psalm 27:10).

Truth be told, I never really understood the real love of a father until I got saved and filled with God's spirit. My God has been a father to me since before I was born, and I thank him so much for loving me when so many times I did not feel loved. I don't think they understood and knew I felt that way, I never told them. I said some things to my mother, but not as much as I wanted to. I didn't want to burden her, and she seemed a bit uncomfortable when I asked about this "so-called father", so I cut it short, and I spoke of it no more.

There were nights I could barely sleep. Trying to figure all this out with it heavy on my mind. I wondered if I ever deserved or would get an explanation or apology EVER!! but I still love and I forgive them. God is still healing my heart. Can you imagine what that felt like all these years? If you do, just know you are not alone ever.

Chapter 4

My Perfect Storm

My mom, my siblings and I moved to West Philly in an apartment when I was 13. We settled there and I met the neighbors down the street. They were very friendly and invited me to go to church with them. I became very close with them and called them my god sisters and their mother my godmother.

We went to church every Sunday and I loved it. After being there for a while I sang in the choir and was pretty much involved in the church. I felt like I was drawn towards the neighbors by God. I was the only one in my house that was going to service and after every sermon that was preached, it was like the pastor was preaching to my situation and I came home filled with the word of God saying, "I am feeling much better about myself, now I feel like I can make it through the week, hallelujah!"

I felt like that because I was being bullied in school and didn't tell my mother. I continued to attend church with my neighbors and it lasted two years. My mom, my siblings and I moved back to North Philly until we found another place to live. I really didn't want to leave. I had grown attached to my neighbors and attending church and did not know where I was going to go to church in North Philly.

I was only 15 and had not made any friends yet... I was bored. I would take a brush and use it as a microphone to sing in the mirror. I had missed going to church and singing. I don't know what to do, the more I was away from church, the more I felt separated from God.

I began roaming the streets making friends and met a boy and the rest was history. I got pregnant at 16. This is when life got real for me.

Chapter 5

Taking Life Serious

I was very sick with morning sickness during my first three months of pregnancy. Five months later my mother found a place for us to live. Finances were tight but we made it through by the help of God. I was about eight months pregnant at this time.

Approaching the age of 17, I soon had my son, March 18th, 1988 a healthy baby boy. My life changed now, and I have a son to raise, not even able to take care of myself. I remember still hanging out with so-called friends partying, experimenting with drugs and alcohol. I became pregnant again within months. My son was not even a year old, and I was feeling scared about what I was going to do. I couldn't take care of the one I had, let alone another. I did not know what to do. Given my situation, a decision was made that I should get an abortion and I remember it was done.

The doctor who prepped me said to me, "don't worry it's not even formed yet." I took another life and felt sad after the procedure again. I just had another fetus that was suctioned out of me not once, but twice in a short period of time.

I asked God years later to forgive me, not knowing what I had let happen during that time. God knows and sees all. I believe things happen for a reason. But I don't think God was very happy about this. He doesn't give us the authority to take a life, that's sin. God is the giver of life. I just knew to give it to God.

I didn't think anything of it at the time because all I thought about was how I was going to take care of them. I just went numb and erased it from my mind. At least I tried to but that did not work. I caught myself thinking of them at times and what they would have grown up to be. Then sometimes I just cried.

We stayed on Bailey Street for a short time after. The house needed some repairs, and the landlord didn't step up. So, one day, my mom told us we were moving. We had to figure out where we were going to live. I had no idea. Finally, my mother and (first) father talked about it and it was settled. We stayed at my (first) father's house. He took us all in and helped us until we found our own place or another place to live. Things seemed to be much better.

We were able to manage better and had a comfortable place to lay our heads until we found places of our own.

Everything was about money growing up with my siblings. I remember them complaining about having to give up most of their money to help out. Times were hard back then; we didn't have much, so everyone had to pitch in. I remember one of them saying, "if I give up all my money, I won't have anything for myself" we laughed but they felt strongly about it.

We used to visit my grandmother often when she was living, she was funny, she used to make me laugh so bad it brought me to tears. She would say "if it is a dollar to be gotten, your mother is gonna get it." And my father used to say, "your mother loves money, anything that involves money." We laughed, I thought nothing of it. I said to myself, "I love money too, it seems like you can't do anything without it." People don't want to be around you when you don't have any money.

I grew up taught that you got to have money to make it out here, you can't do anything without money. Being young, not having much, it was a bit of a struggle. My son was under a year old and I didn't have a job. I wasn't getting any help from my child's father, my mother received benefits for us. She was the one who took care of everything he needed at the time. While my son and I lived with my (first) father, he told me I was old enough now where I could get benefits for my son on my own, but he would have to be removed from my mother's grant and I would have to apply for him on my own. He said, "you need that assistance for you and your son while you are staying with me because you do not have a job and no income, and you need that." I asked, "how do I go about it?" he said, "write a letter telling your mother that you want to take your son off her grant so that you could get benefits for him, now that you are old enough and can receive them while I am living with my son at his house." So, I did just that. I had to move out from the place we were staying to move in with my father. And I needed some kind of income to take care of my son while I was there until I got a job and some housing assistance. Finally, I was able to get assistance for me and my son, and now I could provide what he needed and share expenses for food, or anything needed to compensate for rent.

My (first) (real) dad really didn't ask for anything he just made sure I did the right thing. Making sure my son had food and the things he needed until I was able to stand on my own and find a place for us.

We stayed there awhile, but I don't remember exactly how long.

Chapter 6

Taking Things Slow but Still Going

We moved from there to my aunt's house. She had a room there and allowed my son and I to stay there. I paid rent and I also found a job in the nursing field. My son was old enough to attend daycare. I felt more independent and freer. I had privacy and things were going well.

I would take my son up the street from where we lived where there was a playground and Recreation Center to play on my days off. I would go there regularly. I met a gentleman there that was playing basketball and we became friends. We would meet up there a lot and talk, laugh, and play around. We exchanged numbers and began talking over the phone a lot during late nights. Things got serious. We became as they say, "boyfriend and girlfriend" and as time flew by, we got really involved with one another and I decided to move in with him. I left my aunt's house and moved in with him.

One year later I was pregnant with my second child and shortly after my 3rd. In this relationship as the years went by there was so much, I didn't know or understand. He was older than I was, but I just wanted to feel like I belonged and that I was loved. I have been through so much as a child, I just knew there had to be something better for my life and my children. I continued in the relationship. As time went by, things started to change in the relationship. He started acting different, started staying out overnight while I was pregnant. Telling lies to me that he was working an overnight job. He started being very abusive verbally and I fell into a state of depression and was very sad all the time.

My family didn't like him because he was very disrespectful to them and started being physically abusive later. The times when he had no explanation of where he had been after staying out all night, we would argue and he would curse, call me names, and tell me, "I can get out" and purposely say things to hurt my feelings like, "I just make babies and walk away, so you can leave." But, when I tried to leave, he would fight me so that I could not. I felt trapped as my son watched in fear from a distance. I had nowhere to go, and I couldn't live with any of my relatives because "they had no room." I continued to live in fear for years, with the abuse and all. I was depressed and unhappy and I wanted out of that relationship.

After I had my daughter, I had an escape plan. I would wait until he left to "go to work" as he would say, then we would leave. I found out I could go into a shelter with my children so that when he left, we would be gone, and he would not be able to track us.

When it was clear to go, we left.

We arrived at this shelter where we were seeking assistance for housing until finally, we were placed into a three-story house with rooms, the house happened to be a recovery house, a place for women who had been abused. I was in fear that he would find us but I was informed by the facility that they didn't allow or give out personal information on our whereabouts to anyone who tried to ask. We were safe.

I did not contact him or look for him. Our stay was about six months. During our stay we would visit downtown to the city council's office to get help to push through for our housing. Finally, we got through and sat down with the Councilwoman, who assisted us in the process to search for housing. After that I was blessed to find an apartment and was very excited. I packed up my children and we left. I was kind of nervous and all it was just me and my children making sure we were secure and doing my part. I knew that God was with me and he knew I was done already with the abusive relationship.

Chapter 7

Rededication

In 2015 now at the age of 45, I rededicated my life to Jesus and got baptized and filled with the Holy Spirit. It was April 3rd. Power of his resurrection week. Going forth my life was never the same. I found myself not doing the things I used to do or even desiring to. Even when the enemy tried to push demonic (negative) things into my life. It was so good to know that the power of God rests inside me," what a wonderful feeling," something I couldn't explain, but experienced.

So as time went on in my walk with the Lord, I found a church building that I attended to worship with other believers. Hungry for God I developed an appetite of wanting more, hearing the word, hearing the preachers who were chosen and were helping me in my own situation.

Really desiring and wanting the blessings of spiritual gifts, it was not an option for me or I did not think so at the time. I developed a prayer life talking to God in private in my room just me and him. I talked so much, I wondered if I put him to sleep (LOL), (psalm 121:2-4).

I just had so many questions being a baby in Christ and all. Growing spiritually, I got involved in the church and I joined the praise and worship team. I love singing praises to God. I love singing during my time in the ministry.

I was experiencing a lot of attacks from the enemy of course, he's always roaming around trying to see who he can destroy, (John 10:10). It was then God started opening my eyes to see things as I prayed and asked for understanding, (Proverbs 4:7). I started getting dreams, some were demonic (negative & confusing) and some from God. At this point, I am learning to hear his voice. During this time, I was seeing and hearing, and I wanted to know what I was was seeing and hearing. Was it God or the enemy? What was the message? How do I find out what this all means? What do I do with this information?

I took my questions to the Bishop of the church building I was attending because one of the sisters in church said he was good at teaching people to know God's voice. So, at times I would hear something from God and would go to him or his mother and tell them about a dream I had or what I had heard from God or thought I heard from God.

I started to see more as I fasted and prayed, God opened my eyes so wide, it was overwhelming. The more I went to the

Bishop the more he told me to be sure it was God. Well, the more I went to God the more he showed me. What I saw was true, (1 John 2:27). I saw witchcraft, deceit, flesh rise up, greed, etc. It was like the more I tried to tell the Bishop what God was showing me, I noticed I was being shut down and cut off by the Bishop. This really made me feel bad, unsupported, and not sure where else to turn. I also was confused about how to intrepid what God was showing me. This meant the good that was being shown to me as an anointing was not seen as an anointing, since the people I thought who were supposed to help me were not really helping me. I noticed that the more I talked to them about my spiritual growth the more push back I felt I was getting. I started getting red flags about who I was going to for help.

Now I'm feeling some kind of way, wondering if it was something I did or said. I was just a baby in Christ, hungry for God, and wanting to share my experiences with the church family. I was excited by what God was doing in me. It was like the devil was throwing darts and fire ones at every level. The higher the level the more the devil. I cry out to God a lot, and that was very well known to my church family.

I went to visit this church one Sunday, the pastor was preaching, I was into the message hallelujah and all that then he said, "you see when you always cry, God can't use you" huh? That's all I do is cry out to God, that's my signature (LOL). Maybe I misunderstood him, but I know in scripture we are told to cry out to god. Maybe he meant complaining, I don't know, or I was being told "been there done that" by a certain church member at my own church. I looked at it as they were being sarcastic and prideful.

In the Bible God speaks about crying out to him, (psalm 34:17) and the power in it. It also talks about pride, (Proverbs 8:13). Moving forward there was so much going on in the church building. Jealousy and fakeness, what I did was fast and prayed. God revealed some things to me and told me this was not the place for my soul and that there was an interrupting spirit that would try and stop me from growing spiritually and that I should leave immediately.

I did not reveal this to the Bishop yet, everything I took to him I had to be sure I was hearing from God. So, I waited for confirmation and I asked God to put people in my life that care about my spiritual growth, that are led by his Holy Spirit.

So shortly after, a visitor came to the church one day to visit after service, we had refreshments and food. I walked over to her to greet her with a hug and welcomed her and her daughter. As I finished hugging her, she pulled me back and said, "I have a word for you from the Lord" and she said, "you've been waiting on some money in the mail but have not received it yet. The Lord says, "whatever you release in heaven is released on earth." I said, "WOW." I received it. The Lord spoke through her; it was my confirmation. I was waiting on a check that I did not receive, and I was wondering why it was taking so long. I thanked her for her words.

We sat next to each other. We all ate and talked. She said, "Because you have a loving heart the Lord was able to give me a message for you." I was so amazed, I asked her for her phone number because remember I prayed that God would send someone that cared about my spiritual growth and that was led by his spirit. I said to myself, "Could this be the answer to my prayer?" We exchanged numbers she said she was just visiting and that she does not belong to a church, she goes around ministering and has her own ministry. When I got home, I called her, and we started talking. Praying on the phone for hours she was the first-person God put in my life to show me how to go on a real fast according to the Bible. I mean we were hours a day on the phone praying, studying the Bible, singing, and praising God.

We would wake up at 5:00 AM to pray, if one did not wake up to call, the other did. I went on my first Esther fast (three days no food and no drink). We prayed for my children to be delivered and saved and for God's people and everyone. We also prayed for the check I was waiting for to be released from heaven to earth. In Jesus name.

She taught me a lot and I felt comfortable with sharing with her, and she did also. She told me that I had an anointing on my life and that God is trying to use me for his glory. I remember during this time we were heavy into fasting and praying. I felt this electrifying touch to my body every time I mentioned the name Jesus or talked about him.

First, I thought, "What is that? I'm going to the hospital because it did not stop." and I was scared. I did not know that fasting and praying would take me to a whole new realm in the spirit. Two days on the fast, one day left, I was still holding on by help of the Holy Spirit. I got through the next day and we prayed and broke the fast. It was finished.

Soon after we talked a while, I was getting ready to get dressed and she said let us meet up and go to the whole food store to get some items to change the way we eat. So, leaving out the door before I left, we prayed. She said, "Lord let the check be in the mailbox in Jesus' name." So, when I looked in the mailbox, the check was there. Hallelujah! I shouted and started praising him and thanking him. I was so amazed at not just the check itself but the power of prayer and fasting. What it does, and how it promotes you to new levels in him.

There was so much I experienced in those three days of fasting and seeking the Lord that I could have never imagined such a gift, an anointing, and a check all in one, I was speechless. From then on, I just wanted more of Jesus, and we continued on from time to time speaking on the phone, checking on each other and I just kept thanking God for sending her.

Chapter 8

THE POWER IN PRAYER

I was learning more about God and his word day by day. I was excited. He had me getting up reading scriptures, praying, even meditating, listening for his voice. I loved it and looked forward to it every day. It seemed like after every prayer I prayed, he answered me during this time. I was so caught up in him, like an attic on drugs. I craved for more of him. As I went back to the church I attended, I didn't announce that I was leaving yet, and was not sure how to depart.

After service I went home, took off my church clothes, relaxed sitting before God. Trying to figure out how I was going to announce my departure or get more confirmation. Should I leave or not? A few days past and I ran into a homeless guy who lost his direction and asked if I could help him get back to the shelter, and I said, "yes." This man was 70 years old and suffered from glaucoma, his vision not so great, so I got on the trolley with him and took the paper he had with the address for the shelter a few blocks down where he was staying at the time. We got off at the stop in front of the shelter and he thanked me, and we talked a bit. I prayed, ministered to him, and I invited him to church, and he agreed. I helped and assisted him with things he could not do by himself like shopping for clothes, as well as buy groceries. In addition, he also had an appointment and lab work scheduled so I assisted him to the doctor. Sitting and waiting for him to be called for blood work, a lady walked up to me and said, "God said he has a divine appointment for you, and I think you should be there." She touched me on the shoulder and closed her eyes and said, "Yes, I think you should be there." I took the card she handed to me and told her, "OK." I didn't know her but if God says he had something to tell me then I'm all in. I consulted with the pastor of the church I was attending, and he was against it. I was told to be careful who I let speak into my life.

I went before God and prayed and asked if I was supposed to be at this divine appointment. If I should go or not. Not only did he tell me to go but he told me the lady was his child sent by him. I called her up because we exchanged numbers, she said she would even pick me up and give me a ride. I wasn't driving at the time, so I said, "OK, I'm going." She said, "you will not be disappointed."

It was a prayer breakfast at a hotel. I attended and sure enough God had a message for me. There is one of his chosen vessels, a Judge, Pastor, Coach, anointed woman of God. The word went forth and it was powerful. Afterwards she prayed for people I went before her and she said, "what do you want me to pray for?" I said, "for God's will to be done in my life and to know his instructions for me." She started praying and she said, "after speaking in tongues, communicating with God that God said, "that church is trying to stop you from operating in your gifts." I almost fainted. That was confirmation for me because I was trying to understand why I was always cut off in testimony time and when I tried to voice an opinion or tell what I was hearing from God. It was not acknowledged. Clearly that confirmed I needed to leave that church. Afterwards, I felt at peace and was now ready to move forward. In Jesus name.

I texted the pastor and informed him that I was leaving the church and I did not return. After receiving the word from Pastor Paula, we exchanged numbers and kept in touch and I was still attending her conferences and they were powerful. I then joined another church because Paula did not have a building at that time, she would host meetings at different places touching lives all over the world. I would make myself available to all of her conferences when she posted them. Meanwhile, I started looking for another place of worship. I had become so accustomed to being in a church building with the rest of the saints praising, worshiping, hearing the word of God singing in the choir, it gave me a sense of belonging in the presence of other believers.

After a while of being a member, I started having encounters and seeing different spirits. I kept praying and showing love to the saints being available. The more I prayed, I saw no change. Not that the prayer itself was not heard, but the people must want to change. We are not perfect and there is no perfect church that I know. I continued to pray.

I felt my soul had been tampered with from all the encounters and that was not good. I know God takes us through many experiences to get us to where he needs us to be. I also know he does not play about his souls; he takes them very seriously. This was my exit point. I had grown tired of the familiar and soul slaying spirits. I was spiritually drained. I had to really sit still and get in God's presence to find his place for me. Obviously, my place was not there, I called the pastor and announced my leave. I was blessed and released.

Now I never thought that God was calling me into the Women Aflame Ministry with Judge/Pastor Paula. I thought I was just going to get his word. He was pulling me out of that place into the place he wanted me to be. God cares about souls. I joined and connected back with The Woman Aflame Ministry. I was praying, asking God for help, to send the right people in the faith for my continued learning and serving.

My days were filled with hope. I started understanding more, I was learning how to see, and suddenly stand on my own. Thank God for Jesus.

He set me apart for a reason, that was his plan, (Jeremiah 29:11). Weeks later I started having dreams. I was reading the Bible, I started getting a clear picture, he was speaking to me through his words. Later, in the Ministry, God was really moving. I was made aware of my spiritual gifts under God's anointed led by the Holy Spirit. Things were revealed to me. All good gifts come from him, (James 1:17). I tried to be open and available to him, gleaning and wanting more.

I continued having dreams and, in the dreams, God was revealing some things to me, at times I would pray to God and ask for understanding on why something happened, and he gave me the answers to my questions. Sometimes I would wait a day or two to get the answer and in other times it would be within the hour or instant. When God answers, it is always on his time and you better believe that you will know what you need to know with nothing missing, (Hebrews 11:6).

I developed an appetite for more, wanting to hear more from him every night. I went to bed, I prayed and just sat up meditating waiting to hear from him, (Psalm 27:14). I was so excited, there wasn't a day that went by that I didn't expect to hear from God.

My hunger and thirst caught his attention, (Matthew 5:6). When there was no one I could turn to, I knew to pray and surrender it all to him. Sometimes the enemy may try to come for me and try to discourage me, I send that demonic spirit right to the pit of hell with the sword of the holy spirit. By demonic spirits I mean bad thoughts and negative vibes.

The word of God that keeps me in good spirits, speaks to me in every tough situation in my life. That is why he informs us to renew our minds, (Romans 12:2) and to ponder on things that are pure and praiseworthy. Staying positive is key when you feel like your thoughts are persistently negative.

I realize I have the power through the holy spirit to change atmospheres and lives, (Matthew 5:14-16). And our adversary (the devil), whose job is to steal, kill, and destroy, (John 10:10) will do anything and everything to keep us from reaching our destiny through Christ Jesus.

I have family members who know about God, maybe have backslid, or are not filled with the holy spirit, (Romans 8:9). If they are not trained to fight in warfare prayers, they are easy prey for the devil to come in and set up shop to destroy them and all attached to them. I will continue to pray for my family as long as God gives breath to my lungs. May they be filled with his holy spirit and perfected in his love. For greater is the fire in me than the fire around me.

I have noticed my growth since I have been affiliated with the Woman Aflame Ministry. I have been given a great leader that God chose to use for his glory. Paula A. Patrick, a Coach, Judge, and Pastor has played a huge part in my growth spiritually. God had put her in my life to teach and sharpen my gifts, (Proverbs 27:17), so I may be able to serve others effectively for the Kingdom of God.

I came from sitting in church, listening to the word, and in Bible studies, to being taught how to fight in warfare with prayers, bringing in God's presence by speaking in the spirit, hosting the prayer line, teaching Bible study, and writing my own book and I am still learning and growing. I have had the honor to sit under God's own elect an anointed bearing fruit, for without God we can do nothing.

God said that you will know them by their fruit, (Mathew 7:15). My life was never the same after that, I knew God was taking me higher.

I had a dream I was on the back of an eagle flying extremely high in the sky, it was amazing, who would have known I would have reached this place in God that I am right now, but my desire is to go even higher.

Wherever I go through something, I remember how to fight in prayer and what to ponder on. I try to continue to pray for everyone and to keep my mind off of myself because it's not about me, it's about Jesus and the cost he considered when he laid down his life for not only me but everyone.

What I do know is that while I am living for him, since he died for me, I know he will take care of me while I'm praying and serving others, (Romans 5:8).

I thank God we are saved by grace and I thank him for Jesus. This life is still a battle, but I keep my eyes looking towards the hills where my help comes from, (Psalm 121:1-2). And I try to stay with the heart of praise with the Holy Spirit guiding me. We are not perfect, but the perfector will one day make everything perfect, (Jesus). For we are living in a dying world and I know many are lost.

God needs me for such a time as this. For many are called but few are chosen, (Mathew 22:14), and I am glad he chose me. Where God has placed me, I will stand as his chosen vessel for his glory. I have come too far to turn back now, (Luke 9:62) so I will keep moving forward in Christ Jesus that he will continue to be in my life all the days of my life.

I'm no longer in bondage of my past, (Galatians 4:7). I am filled with his spirit and baptized with his Holy Spirit. I am born again, (John 3:3) and this is a gift from God. All those times I was crying in pain, God was right there, (psalm 126:5). He never left me. He has a reason and a plan for my life.

I look forward to serving him every day of my life, without doubt. There is only one way, and that is towards heaven, "This life doesn't owe me nothing, I got everything from God in me that I need." This will be done, in Jesus's name.

I am free of bad relationships, free of drugs, alcohol, and I am happy in Christ Jesus. Thank God for covering my children in the blood of Jesus. He is continuously working in their lives. "Many are the afflictions of the righteous but it's the lord who delivers them out of them all." (Psalm 34:19) who the son of man has made free is free indeed, (John 8:36).

I'm Free! Prepared by God for Greater!

Chapter 9

Daily Connection Options

- Wake up say good morning to God and thank him for the day
- Pray
- Ask the holy spirit to lead the way
- Go about the day in praise and worship
- Find time to sit, read, listen to sermons
- Study the word of god
- Meditate and listen for instructions
- Be obedient, if you're not sure ask for confirmation from God

Conclusion

He turned my mess into a message

He turned my fears into faith

He turned my pain into power

Through my pass came my purpose

No Cross, no crown

I am an overcomer

Because of God's grace, I am saved through Christ Jesus, to him be the glory forever

Amen

GRACE

***G**od's*

***R**iches*

***A**t*

***C**hrist*

***E**xpense*

Acknowledgements

My thank you poem to God:

I thank you lord everyday,
For how you encourage me to pray,
When I am lost for words to say,
Your holy spirit leads the way,
"Yes, my daughter it is ok",
I will lead you, guide you, in my way.
Your crying out was not in vain,
I see it all, your hurt and pain.
I took you through to strengthen you too,
All this was my purpose for you.
I opened your eyes for you to see,
My love, my joy, your place in me.
I thank you lord for all you do,
My love, my life, my being in you.

ABOUT THE AUTHOR

A mother of three and a grandmother of five Nadine is looking forward to her next book hoping to touch, encourage, and inspire people all over the world that are struggling with mental, physical, and emotional abuse. Professionally Nadine Sallins has 21 years' experience in the nursing field and has a passion for helping others. She has dedicated her life to giving and helping those that are less fortunate. Nadine was born 1970 in the state of Pennsylvania and is currently a resident in the borough of Sharon Hill.

Thank you for reading my book:

I really appreciate all your feedback and would love to hear your thoughts on the book.

Hearing from you helps me know if I helped and encouraged my readers. I appreciate a helpful and honest review on amazon so that I know what your thoughts were on the book.

God Bless You!

Nadine Sallins